THE LITTLE GUIDE TO

GUCCI

Published in 2024 by OH!
An Imprint of Welbeck Non-Fiction Limited,
part of Welbeck Publishing Group.
Offices in London – 20 Mortimer Street, London W1T 3JW
and Sydney – Level 17, 207 Kent St, Sydney NSW 2000 Australia
www.welbeckpublishing.com

ISBN 978-1-80069-621-1

Compiled and written by: Glenys Johnson
Editorial: Matt Tomlinson and Saneaah Muhammad
Project manager: Russell Porter
Production: Rachel Burgess

A CIP catalogue record for this book is available from the British Library

Printed in Italy

10 9 8 7 6 5 4 3 2

THE LITTLE GUIDE TO

GUCCI

STYLE TO LIVE BY

Unofficial and Unauthorized

CONTENTS

INTRODUCTION

The Gucci name travels far beyond the title of an iconic fashion house. Gucci has come to represent a juggernaut that has left an indelible mark on the fashion world, with its rich history, visionary leadership and influential styles.

The Gucci family can be traced back to 15th-century Florence, but the modern brand emerged in Florence in 1921, cementing Italian design on the fashion map. Since then, Gucci has evolved into a global powerhouse, captivating high society and Hollywood alike. With famous fans from Elizabeth Taylor to Demi Moore, the brand had remained consistently desirable for over a century.

Passed down from father to sons, and with a fascinating and almost scandalous family history, Gucci's story is one of resilience, creativity and innovation, weathering challenges and setbacks to emerge as a symbol of Italian luxury.

From the creation of the "Flora Scarf" designed for Princess of Monaco, Grace Kelly herself, to the emergence of the interlocking G logo, red and green stripe, opulent luggage and diamond print logo,

Gucci's multitude of signature elements are instantly recognized worldwide.

Whether it's the Gucci loafer being placed in the Metropolitan Museum of Art's permanent collection or an entire museum dedicated to the fashion house in Florence, Gucci has become the epitome of luxury, synonymous with sophistication and elegance and talked about by actors, singers, models and all other manner of celebrities alike. Gucci's enduring allure and ability to capture the hearts and attention of fashion enthusiasts worldwide make the label one of the most iconic and influential fashion houses to date, with esteemed figures such as Tom Ford, Frida Giannini and Alessandro Michele creatively directing the brand down different visionary paths.

This little guide to the iconic fashion house is full of quotes from designers, fans and the family themselves, alongside the history of the brand and facts about the company throughout the years. Whether you're a Gucci aficionado or a longing window-shopper, this book is the ultimate guide to one of fashion's most iconic names.

CHAPTER
ONE

THE EARLY DAYS

THE STORY OF GUCCI DATES
BACK TO MARCH 26, 1881.
GUCCIO GUCCI WAS BORN TO
ITALIAN GOODS MAKERS IN
FLORENCE, ITALY, AND BY THE
TIME HE WAS JUST 19, HE HAD
TRAVELLED TO LONDON AND WAS
WORKING AS A PORTER AT THE
PRESTIGIOUS SAVOY HOTEL.

His time in the United Kingdom was where his admiration for luxurious luggage developed and ultimately led him to create luggage designs of his own.

Gucci is not a fashion or a design house; it was always a trademark.

Maurizio Gucci (son of Rodolfo Gucci, grandson of Guccio Gucci).

He returned to Florence
to learn the skills of
the trade at the leather
manufacturer, Franzi.

During this time Guccio
met 24-year-old dressmaker
Aida Calvelli and married
her in 1901.

The couple had five children:
Ugo, Grimalda, Enzo, Aldo, Vasco
and Rodolfo. Enzo sadly passed
away as a child.

The remaining sons went on to play key roles in the house of Gucci, although daughter Grimalda was controversially left out of much of the business endeavours over the years.

My father, and Guccio before him, always intended the business to be family-run, and that meant staying in Florence. Of course, times change and we all move along accordingly, but there is much to be said for legacy and tradition.

Patricia Gucci (daughter of Aldo Gucci, granddaughter of Guccio Gucci).

Classiq, September 2016.

By 1921, Guccio became confident enough to step out and start building the foundation of his own brand.

He opened his first shop,
**Azienda Individuale
Guccio Gucci**,
on the famous
Via della Vigna Nuova
in Florence.

Guccio's aim was to cater to the wealthiest of the population, importing fine luggage from across Europe that he offered alongside his own designs.

Soon, his production line expanded to manufacturing horse riding accessories, drawing in the equestrian-loving elite.

> **"**
>
> As a designer, he aimed to create pieces that were everlasting and acknowledged that the highest standards of craftsmanship would garner a higher price tag.
> The foundation that Guccio built for Gucci can be seen within the brand's famous signatures and commitment to total luxury.
>
> **"**

Mina Dragani

L'Officiel, March 2023.

As the Gucci brand developed, Guccio's sons began assisting across all areas of the label, turning Gucci into a true family business.

This family involvement would later caused serious turmoil, and ultimately led to many members of Gucci family going to court a few decades later.

The brand's Florentine identity carries an important symbolism that must be maintained.

Patricia Gucci

Classiq, September 2016.

By the 1930s, Guccio had built quite the name for himself in the world of leather bags. His success would be credited to his commitment to premium craftsmanship.

By opening his own Tuscany workshop, Guccio could oversee production and ensure his vision of British-influenced quality goods with a traditional Italian tone.

Quality is remembered long
after price is forgotten.

Aldo Gucci (son of Guccio Gucci).

CHAPTER
TWO

CEMENTING
THE BRAND

AT THE AGE OF 20, ALDO GUCCI
JOINED HIS FATHER'S BUSINESS.
HE PLAYED A KEY ROLE IN
DEVELOPING THE LABEL FURTHER
AND CREATING ITS ICONIC
BRANDING.

IN 1933, ALDO CREATED THE
INTERLOCKING GG LOGO,
AND BY 1934 THE LOGO WAS
BEING USED ON LUGGAGE FROM
THE BRAND.

> **The celebrated double-G has come to represent more than success... Gucci means prestige and good taste.**

Laird Borrelli-Persson

"Everything You Need to Know About the House of Gucci Before Watching House of Gucci", *Vogue*, November 24, 2021.

The ambitions to grow to become one of the world's most coveted names behind leather goods had to be temporarily paused in the 1930s as the League of Nations severely restricted the import of leather into Italy.

But even at this time, the Gucci brand understood the power of adaptability.

The family business quickly began developing alternative materials for crafting bags and accessories, looking to hemp to display Gucci's first signature print, a diamond print in a dark brown colour.

The "Diamante" print
quickly became a staple across
Gucci's creations and still
remains one of the
most recognizable aspects of
the brand today.

66

Elegance is like manners. You can't be polite only on Wednesday or Thursday. If you are elegant, you should be every day of the week.

99

Aldo Gucci

The equestrian influence became
a key trademark for the Italian
label, with the company producing
leather saddles and other
horseback-riding accessories,
alongside luggage, in the 1920s.

Gucci moved into fashion in 1932, with their first leather shoes.

The iconic bamboo handle, released in 1947, was a solution to the scarcity of other materials caused by the Fascist occupation in Italy at the time, but this unique alteration would help cement Gucci further into the wardrobes of the most stylish Europeans of the time.

> **"**
> Gucci was one of the pioneers
> of the international fashion
> boom, combining centuries-old
> Florentine artisanship with
> modern snob appeal.
> **"**

The Gazette, October 1998.

Sadly, Guccio Gucci passed away at age 72, in 1953.

By the 1950s,
Gucci had reached
the "Big Apple".

Gucci's move into the American market quickly made it a forerunner in the world of Italian sophistication, and some of the biggest celebrities of the time embraced it with open arms.

As Gucci expanded in the 60s and 70s, the iconic "GG" monogram print became sought-after worldwide.

The Gucci GG logo is the jewel
in the Gucci crown.

Alek Rose

Highsnobiety, August 2022.

In the 1960s, Gucci expanded their shops throughout the United States and European capitals.

A-list stars flocked to the brand for stylish goods, including Hollywood's very own Grace Kelly and First Lady Jackie Kennedy.

These stars would not only act as an advertisement for Gucci but also inspire some of the brand's most famous patterns and designs.

President John F. Kennedy is noted to have referred to Aldo Gucci as the first Italian Ambassador to fashion.

Aldo was awarded an honorary degree by the City University of New York as a way to recognise his philanthropic contributions over the years.

> **As Gucci grew in popularity, it became synonymous with high-class elegance and glamour.**

Irene Anna Kim and Jay Reed

Business Insider, March 2021.

The origin story of the Flora print is set in 1966 when Grace Kelly walked into the Gucci store in Milan.

Rodolfo Gucci promised the actress-turned-princess a custom piece, inspired by her love for florals.

Rodolfo quickly commissioned illustrator Vittorio Accornero for a special design for Ms. Kelly – and thus the Flora print was born.

> "The princess asked for a scarf, but Rodolfo Gucci himself said he didn't have something beautiful enough for such a special guest... The following day Accornero arrived with a painting representing nine bunches of wild flowers with insects jumping from a bouquet to another. It was the beginning of a legend."

Alessandro Masetti

The Fashion Commentator, June 2012.

The Flora was the first of a range of prints designed by Accornero for the Italian luxury label.

The delicate design would soon find itself sprawled across everything from scarves to mini dresses and, later, handbags and menswear accessories.

The nine bouquets illustrated on the print are composed of a variety of flowers, including tulips, lilies, poppies, daffodils and irises.

The insects include butterflies, grasshoppers, bees and dragonflies.

In the 1970s, Gucci entered the world of luxury fragrances with the scent Gucci No.1.

Since then, over 100 fragrances have been created under the Gucci name.

The craftsmanship, the richness of colours and intricacy of Vittorio Accornero's floral and insect designs makes them highly sought after.

Maria Luisa Frisa

The curator behind Gucci's 2023 Gucci Cosmos, quoted in *The Financial Times*, September 2023.

In 1979, Gucci partnered with car manufacturer Cadillac to release a limited-edition run of its Seville model, adorned with Gucci-branded leather seating and red and green stripe details.

Only 300 cars were produced.

CHAPTER
THREE

THE FAMILY TROUBLES

BEYOND THE DEDICATION TO QUALITY, GUCCI'S HISTORY CAN ALSO BE EXPLORED THROUGH THE DRAMA AND TURMOIL AMONG THE GUCCI FAMILY ITSELF...

The real troubles began in the early 1980s, when Rodolfo Gucci, son of Guccio Gucci, died at age 70.

He had played a key role in the global expansion of Gucci since he joined the company full-time in 1953.

It's a timeless story. There are
lessons in it, like blood should
be thicker than water. And
unfortunately, in this case, it wasn't.

Sara Gay Forden

*The House of Gucci: A Sensational Story of Murder, Madness,
Glamour, and Greed, 2001.*

By this time, the brand had been suffering hardship at the hands of Aldo Gucci for years.

Maurizio, son of Rodolfo, was dissatisfied with his uncle Aldo's mass production approach, which he felt cheapened the brand's luxury identity. He began legal battles to push Aldo out of the business and take over the company.

A lengthy battle between Aldo and Maurizio followed over the ownership of the Gucci brand.

In 1986, Aldo pleaded guilty to tax evasion and served a year in a penitentiary in Florida and Maurizio fled to Switzerland after being accused of forging his father's signature to avoid paying inheritance taxes.

He was later acquitted.

66

The family drama is as
remorseless as a Greek tragedy.

99

Justine Picardie

The Telegraph, November 2011.

In 1992, Gucci served papers to Dapper Dan, a Harlem fashion designer who used the label's logos on counterfeit goods. Two decades later, Gucci faced criticism for copying one of his designs.

In 2018, following years of mutual admiration and imitation, Gucci collaborated with the streetwear icon and sponsored the reopening of Dapper Dan's studio as an appointment-only boutique.

The Gucci family's internal conflicts and power struggles were highly publicized, ultimately resulting in the end of the family's ties to the company.

Maurizio's decision to sell the remainder of his shares to Investcorp in 1993 marked the conclusion of the family's involvement in the company.

> "
>
> In the mid-90s, a number of the people Maurizio had hired during his attempt to revive the brand actually did manage to steer it into a new, wildly successful era – but only after he'd tapped out.
>
> "

Danielle Cohen

"The True Story That Inspired the House of Gucci", *The Cut*, November 2021.

Alongside the turmoil among the Gucci family, trouble was also brewing in Maurizio's love life.

In 1970, he married Italian socialite Patrizia Reggiani. Rodolfo, Maurizio's father, referred to her as "a social climber who had nothing in mind but money". By 1985, their marriage had disintegrated to the point of Maurizio calling it off.

She confessed once in a television
interview that she would rather
'weep in a Rolls-Royce than be
happy on a bicycle'.

Sara Gay Forden

*The House of Gucci: A Sensational Story of Murder, Madness,
Glamour, and Greed, 2001.*

This initiated a decade of resentment and jealousy from Patrizia, leading her to hire a hitman to kill Maurizio, a violent act that was carried out on March 27, 1995.

Patrizia was found guilty of
Mautizio's murder in 1998 and
was sentenced to 29 years in
prison, though she was released
in 2016 after a reduced sentence
for "good behaviour".

> **"**
>
> [Maurizio] had a big smile and was very elegant — and profoundly Italian. He was proud and obsessed about Made in Italy, and thought it was a trademark of its own. **"**

Cristina Malgara

Former member of the Gucci PR team, *WWD*, March 2021.

In 2001, journalist Sara Gay Forden turned the story into a book, appropriately titled *House of Gucci*.

Award-winning film director Ridley Scott saw the silver-screen appeal of the family drama and adapted the book into a film of the same name in 2021.

Aldo Gucci's heirs notably responded to the film, condemning the depiction of the family and stating: "The film carries a narrative that is far from accurate."

The Guccis were a great family. I ask forgiveness for all their mistakes. Who doesn't make mistakes?

Sara Gay Forden

The House of Gucci: A Sensational Story of Murder, Madness, Glamour, and Greed, 2001.

CHAPTER
FOUR

KEY STYLES

GUCCI'S RELATIONSHIP WITH
ITS HISTORY ISN'T SIMPLE. BUT
REGARDLESS OF WHO IS RUNNING
THE SHOW, THERE ARE A FEW
KEY STYLES THAT REMAIN
A MAINSTAY, SEASON AFTER
SEASON.

Transformed, renamed and reimagined through the lenses of various periods, Gucci's staple styles provide a powerful sentiment to the strength of the Italian fashion house and its unrelenting chokehold on the fashion world at large.

Following his father's passing in 1953, Aldo Gucci set out to create a style to pay tribute to Guccio and his love for equestrian style.

This led to one of Gucci's most significant creations for decades.

Horsebit loafer

The Horsebit loafer helped infuse the once-utilitarian metal clasping with the world of luxury fashion in an entirely new way.

It was rumoured that Aldo wanted to mark the Gucci brand on the leather loafer styles that inspired him.

"

What do late former US president
George H. W. Bush, '60s muse
Jane Birkin and rapper Wiz Khalifa
all have in common? Despite
their vastly differing personal styles
and occupations, they have all
been spotted in a pair of Gucci
horsebit loafers.

"

Leah Dolan

CNN.com, June 2023.

The loafer has won the hearts of history's most fashionable names, including Sophia Loren and Jane Birkin, who sported the leather style in the 60s and 70s.

The Gucci Horsebit loafer
is the only footwear style
in the permanent collection
at New York's Metropolitan
Museum of Modern Art.

"

Originally for men, the shoe
was soon followed by women's
versions, and both won the hearts
– and lire – of newly solvent
Italians enamored with the design
objects that they associated with
their country's postwar rebirth.

"

Horacio Silva

W Magazine, October 2023.

In recent years, Hailey Bieber, Bella Hadid and Dakota Johnson have all been spotted with the iconic footwear on their feet, confirming that the Horsebit remains as coveted now as it ever was.

The metal hardware with its double ring and bar is a nod to the brand's captivation and history with the equestrian lifestyle.

First used on loafers, it continued to remain a staple icon on handbags a few years later.

"

The Horsebit's impact went beyond sales figures. It was in step with a changing, more liberal approach to conventional dress codes… Understated yet easily recognizable from a distance, it exuded carefree glamour, with just a hint of status signaling.

"

Horacio Silva

W Magazine, October 2023.

The Gucci Bamboo bag

The Gucci Bamboo bag (originally known simply as the 0633 model), was originally released in 1947, prompted by Italy's post-war response to a leather shortage.

Gucci improvised by crafting the bag's handle and turn-lock closure from bamboo, a Japanese material that was readily available, durable and lightweight.

The design would not only address the scarcity of traditional raw materials but also led to the creation of an iconic accessory in the process.

Names like Ingrid Bergman helped make the style a hit by featuring it in *Viaggio in Italia*.

The slick yet earthy article has since become one of the brands most recognisable features. It is both timeless and sophisticated, elegant yet edgy.

Wonderland, January 2022.

The Gucci Bamboo has remained popular for over 75 years and is a notable favourite amongst various modern fashion icons including Harry Styles, Alexa Chung, Elle Fanning and Beyonce.

Gucci has always represented great design and contemporary lifestyle.

Marco Bizzarri

Fashion Network, January 2016.

The Gucci Horsebit bag

Gucci Horsebit bag has sat atop Gucci's most iconic handbag lists since its inception in 1955.

Tom Ford reinvented the Horsebit bag as a daring clutch with studded exotic leathers and a chain strap, worn alongside more provocative outfits.

> "
> There have been endless iterations of the luxury Italian brand's emblem, but no stamp feels quite as iconic as the house's Horsebit. Introduced in 1955, the equestrian-adjacent hardware has enjoyed an enduring place in Gucci's identity.
> "

Ella O'Keeffe

Russh, June 2023.

The coveted shoulder bag design was reintroduced by Alessandro Michele in 2019 for the Gucci 2020 Cruise collection, staying true to its original form and design with a saddle silhouette and sleek finish.

Gucci-loving A-listers including Halle Bailey and Julia Garner are known to reach for the Horsebit style frequently.

The Horsebit bag was reinvented in 2023 in Demetra, a vegan alternative to leather developed by Gucci, to further the house's sustainability efforts.

The Jackie bag

Created in 1961, the Jackie bag (originally called the Constance) is known for its hobo shape and vintage-inspired charm.
The bag gained popularity when it was photographed on the arm of style icon Jackie Kennedy Onassis throughout the 60s and 70s.

> "
>
> Like the enduring allure of the woman it's named after, the Jackie is a bag that will never go out of style.
>
> "

Lilah Ramzi

Vogue, October 2023.

In 2020, Gucci's creative director, Alessandro Michele, reimagined the bag, presenting the Jackie 1961 with a genderless attitude and multi-styling.

The bag was resized in mini, small and medium versions, and was updated to include a minimal silhouette and a variety of colour options, reflecting a new relevance for contemporary fashion.

The Soho Disco bag

As a more modern Gucci gem, the Soho Disco quickly became a widely loved icon when it was introduced by Frida Giannini in 2012. The camera-style crossbody bag acted as a gateway to the Gucci world, designed with pebbled calfskin leather and embossed with the interlocking double-G logo.

The bag was originally available in a variety of saturated colours to suit any occasion and to wear with any outfit, allowing the Gucci brand to appear more accessible for more people to enjoy.

The piece quickly reached It-bag status, appearing on downtown girls and boys around Soho... as the ultimate hands-free accessory.

Lilah Ramzi

Vogue, October 2023.

The Soho Disco was designed to be an easily worn and deceptively spacious bag, allowing it to transform from a day-time bag to a night-time accessory.

CHAPTER
FIVE

TOM FORD

IN 1990, TEXAS-BORN TALENT
TOM FORD WAS APPOINTED AS
HEAD OF WOMEN'S READY TO
WEAR AT GUCCI.

WITH A CV UNLIKE ANYONE
WHO HAD HELD THE POSITION
BEFORE, FORD PROVED TO BE
JUST WHAT THE LABEL NEEDED TO
BRING IT OUT OF THE LULL IT
HAD BEEN EXPERIENCING.

You should put on the best version of yourself when you go out in the world because that is a show of respect to the other people around you.

Tom Ford

AnOther Magazine, March 2011.

Ford's background in the film industry meant his commitment to the aesthetics and photography behind the brand was just as powerful as the designs seen on storefronts and catwalks.

That era was so sexy, empowering, elegant. A defining moment for the house; game-changing for fashion.

Marie Blanchet

FT.com, September 2023.

A mere two years after accepting the role in the label's womenswear department, Ford was promoted to overseeing the fragrance, advertising and design of the Gucci stores.

He soon rose to a position that allowed his talents to beam even brighter: Creative Director.

The Gucci woman – you know what she's after.

Tom Ford

Ford's first collections for the brand were drenched in sexy 70s influences that immediately captured the attention of fashion critics and celebrities who praised him for breathing new life into the catwalk shows.

"

He championed all-out sexiness, putting risqué silhouettes and suggestive fabrics centre stage.

Alice Cary

Vogue, January 2023.

With each collection, Ford's dedication to shaking up the fashion scene strengthened.

Half-naked models adorned catwalks, and Gucci's advertisements consistently grabbed headlines for their risqué imagery depicting not-so-subtle hints at models engaging in sex acts.

Some of the period's biggest models were spotted in Gucci's ads under Ford's direction.

Kate Moss and Georgina Grenville were depicted in suggestive poses beside shirtless male models, with the Gucci G-string as a staple in these provocative campaigns.

The beautiful people no longer cared about a label that had sold its soul to the tea-towel makers. They wanted glamour, luxury, excess – and Ford gave it to them.

Catherine Hayward

GQ, March 2012.

115

Gucci's Genius Jeans were awarded the title of the World's Most Expensive Jeans in the Guinness Book of World Records in 1998.

The style was sold for $3,134 USD at the time.

In 2003, the fashion house launched its most controversial imagery to date, with model Carmen Kass revealing the Gucci G shaved into her pubic hair, revealing it to the camera.

An era like Tom's at Gucci will always be relevant because it really set the bar for everyone in fashion. Then and now.

Alexis Novak

Vogue, January 2023.

By the time Ford left Gucci in 2004, he had transformed the brand's reputation and relevance in the fashion world in an almost immeasurable way.

During
Ford's tenure,
the value of Gucci
went up by
an impressive
90%.

His work is often credited for saving Gucci from fading into the sea of struggling heritage brands who lost their way.

Ford's impact was felt through Gucci and the wider fashion world even decades later.

At that time everyone was
branding, branding, branding...
and I thought how far can branding
go? It was provocative but,

without wishing to sound
pretentious, I like to think there's
a bit of reason and intelligence
behind my provocation.

"

Tom Ford

Vogue France, August 2019.

> **I think Gucci is one of those brands that is really open-minded to a lot of new and fresh and fun ideas.**

A$AP Rocky

Dazed, October 2023.

You really do get to give
the world your taste once – and
I did that at Gucci.

Tom Ford

i-D, December 2021.

CHAPTER SIX

FRIDA GIANNINI

IN 2002, FRIDA GIANNINI
JOINED GUCCI AS ITS DESIGN
DIRECTOR FOR THE HANDBAG
DEPARTMENT.

TWO YEARS LATER, SHE WENT
ON TO RUN THE WOMEN'S
READY-TO-WEAR RANGE
BEFORE HOLDING THE TITLE OF
CREATIVE DIRECTOR IN 2006.

Can you imagine a world where all
did exactly the same thing? Gucci
can never be an intellectual brand…
The DNA we're based on, the
glamour, it's always been there since

the Gucci family decided to go out of Italy and open the first stores in America. This glamorous world, which is still there.

"

Frida Giannini

i-D, February 2014.

Giannini's ethos moved the brand away from Ford's approach of pushing limits and sensual aesthetics and shifted the focus back to Gucci's heritage.

After Ford's dedication to creative aspirational styles and elevating the Gucci name, Giannini aimed to develop Gucci into a brand that more people could have a piece of.

I don't think that being innovative means making only strange or weird things that you would never see in the street.

Frida Giannini

W Magazine, August 2010.

Giannini believed that the way forward involved re-establishing the feminine elements that Gucci had strayed from under Ford's helm.

Flora prints, bamboo bags and the double G logo saw themselves thrust into the spotlight in a way that was more focused on the commercial success than the divisive spirit that Ford helped infuse into the brand.

Gucci doesn't belong in a mall,
it belongs in a museum.

Rodolfo Gucci

House of Gucci, 2021.

For Gucci's first
TV advertisement in 2008,
Frida Giannini commissioned
award-winning director
David Lynch to bring the Gucci
by Gucci fragrance to life.

The piece featured models
Raquel Zimmerman,
Natasha Poly and Freja
Beha Erichsen.

66

Under Ford, Gucci employees maintained an antiseptic, monochromatic look. Giannini turned up, on her first day, with platinum-blond hair and a vivid print blouse: a moment that came to be known, in company lore, as The Romans Have Arrived.

99

Lauren Collins

W Magazine, August 2010.

To mark the fashion house's 90th anniversary, a museum dedicated to Gucci was unveiled in its hometown of Florence in 2011.

The Gucci Garden, as it is known, features some of Gucci's most iconic pieces, an impressive shop, a restaurant and a cafe/cocktail bar.

Duality: the ability to look ahead
without losing sight of the past.

Frida Giannini

On what she felt defined contemporary Italian fashion and her
approach to design at Gucci, *Dazed*, March 2012.

Critics were quick to speculate about Giannini's motives, with queries over whether her intent was really to revive Gucci's heritage or if she was merely trying to cater to younger audiences and following trends of the time.

I don't like to treat a piece of clothing like an object of art because I don't consider myself an artist. I'm a designer.

Frida Giannini

Harper's Bazaar, February 2011.

> **"**
>
> The Gucci woman can be the equestrian woman, the woman in the suit the woman in the flowy bohemian dress or the couture woman.
>
> **"**

Blake Lively

In 2013, Gucci launched the global campaign Gucci CHIME.

Alongside Salma Hayek Pinault and Beyoncé Knowles-Carter, the gender equality initiative has raised nearly 21.5 million USD for over 500 projects across the globe.

Things reportedly took a turn for the worse when internal feuds related to Giannini's romantic relationship with Gucci CEO Patrizio di Marco came to a head in 2014, resulting in both of them leaving the house of Gucci at short notice.

My philosophy is to do wearable things that people want to buy... I think it's correct for me to create something that has exclusivity, that is really Gucci, but at the same time is something I want to see on people.

Frida Giannini

i-D, February 2014.

CHAPTER
SEVEN

ALESSANDRO MICHELE

IN 2015, GUCCI SHARED THAT A NEW NAME WOULD BE TAKING OVER GIANNINI'S ROLE AT THE FASHION HOUSE.

THE TITLE OF CREATIVE DIRECTOR WOULD GO TO ROMAN DESIGNER ALESSANDRO MICHELE.

Why should I look for someone else
when he can translate the heritage
— and when the values of Gucci
are in his veins?

Gucci CEO Marco Bizzarri

On his rationale for selecting the relatively unknown name for the
coveted role of Creative Director, *Vogue*, 2015.

Fashion is not just about buying a bag. It's a big audience, it's a stage, and I hope people see what is happening here. Humanity needs a new energy, doing the same thing for 100 years doesn't make sense.

Alessandro Michele

i-D, October 2020.

With a mere five days to prepare Gucci's Autumn/Winter 2015 menswear show, Michele quickly stirred the fashion world.

Journalist Lauren Indvik of *Fashionista* referred to the new collection as…

Vintage-y mink coats, androgynous suiting, wallpaper florals, tilted berets and geek-chic glasses, they evoked not sex but the rag-tag glamour of a Wes Anderson film.

Fashionista, December 2015.

When Gucci started, it was another age. If you bought a Gucci bag, you belonged to the jet set. The jet set doesn't exist anymore. I'm trying to speak to the world, to everyone.

Alessandro Michele

AnOther Magazine, February 2018.

Michele's fresh take on the Italian fashion house quickly infused a maximalist tone with bright and bold colourways and an eclectic infusion of patterns that couldn't be ignored.

Gucci made history in June 2016 when it became the first-ever fashion brand to host a runway show in the iconic Westminster Abbey, where it showcased its Cruise 2017 collection.

Sometimes people think that fashion is just a good dress, but it's not. It's a bigger reflection of history and social change and very powerful things.

Alessandro Michele

Vogue, 2019.

Michele made his mark by turning a period of struggle for Gucci into a new start, gaining newfound respect from younger generations while still maintaining the respect of Gucci as a luxury brand.

Gucci is a brand that is full of past, but you can ignore the past, because it's also now.

Alessandro Michele

Antidote, 2016.

Fashion is not about product; it's about an interesting idea that you can't resist buying into.

Alessandro Michele

WWD, May 2016.

A key theme that Michele brought back to Gucci was looking at the world through a post-gender lens.

Many believe that Ford's legacy of playing with traditionally feminine and masculine elements was lost during Giannini's reign, but Michele made it clear that he was determined to bring back this fundamental element for Gucci.

Removing the gendered element of the collections was one of Michele's first big moves for the label, garnering many headlines and praise from younger critics.

"

Michele has held a mirror up to our world, reflecting the tension, the sexuality, the fragility of being a man in modern times back to us with passion, rigor, symbolism and love.

"

Steff Yotka

GQ, October 2019.

"

Alessandro Michele is in the spotlight as the Pied Piper of change – a risk-taker and revolutionary who has not so much wiped the slate clean at Gucci as doodled all over it, coloured it in, stuck sequins on it, and tied it up with a grosgrain bow.

"

Sarah Mower

Summarizing the shift in tone in the spring/summer 2016 show, *Vogue*, 2015.

Michele revolutionized the brand by introducing more extravagant patterns and designs.

Among his iconic creations is the Dionysus bag, with aged metal tiger-head hardware inspired by a Greek god with the same name.

The myth suggests that Zeus sent Dionysus a tiger to cross the river Tigris.

"

We are not just an atelier anymore
and I'm not just a fashion designer.
Gucci occupies the same reference
point as a pop band for a lot
of young people. Gucci is like
Woodstock in the imagination. **"**

Alessandro Michele

i-D, October 2020.

In 2017, Michele made headlines by eliminating fur from the brand's products completely.

This was a move made to help reduce its impact on both animals and the environment.

Michele continued to make earth-conscious movements when, in the fall of 2019, Gucci announced that its Spring/Summer 2020 runway show in Milan would be carbon neutral.

I think that the era of being masculine only if you have a specific suit – it's over. Completely over.

Alessandro Michele

GQ, October 2019.

After years of friendship, Harry Styles and Alessandro Michele teamed up to release the Gucci HA HA HA collection in November 2022.

The line-up featured a range of graphic tees, a Prince of Wales check coat, pastel flares and various tailored styles.

When the world looks back at
the tumultuous teenage years of
twenty-first century fashion, the
appointment of Alessandro Michele
as creative director of Gucci will
be pointed to as the moment the
fashion world felt a seismic shift
under its sartorial feet.

Jessica Michault

Antidote, March 2016.

As one of his final moves, the Roman designer led the launch of Off the Grid, Gucci's eco-conscious range that featured organic, recycled and bio-based materials and appeared in a virtual campaign starring Jane Fonda, Lil Nas X and more.

As the lines between luxury and street continue to blur, Gucci seems less interested in upholding that boundary and more interested in embracing the pockets of culture it has managed to reach over the last 100 years.

Weiqi Yap

Vogue, 2022.

Gucci made headlines with its FW22 presentation when it revealed a selection of styles made in collaboration with sportswear brand adidas.

To the great pleasure of fashion lovers across the globe, the full collection was launched in June 2022 and affectionately referred to as "Guccididas".

CHAPTER
EIGHT

SABATO DE SARNO

IN FEBRUARY 2023, GUCCI ANNOUNCED A NEW VISIONARY WOULD BE LEADING THE CREATIVE DIRECTION: A NEOPOLITAN DESIGNER BY THE NAME OF SABATO DE SARNO.

DE SARNO HAD EXPERIENCE HEADING VARIOUS DEPARTMENTS FOR DOLCE & GABBANA, PRADA AND VALENTINO, BUT GUCCI WAS A NEW CHALLENGE.

It's a very Italian brand with a huge heritage. Italian in craftsmanship, Italian in taste, and we lost that I think. I want to bring it back. Italianity is part of my story, for sure.

Sabato De Sarno

Vogue, September 2023.

I am certain that through Sabato's deep understanding and appreciation for Gucci's unique legacy, he will lead our creative teams with a distinctive vision that will help write this exciting next chapter, reinforcing the House's fashion authority while capitalizing on its rich heritage.

Marco Bizzarri

Gucci's president and CEO, *Vogue*, 2023.

Gucci is a big opportunity for me.
I'm conscious of that and I want
to give opportunities to other
people... I want to discover people
and help them to shine.

Sabato De Sarno

Vogue, September 2023.

The first campaign released under De Sarno's helm saw Daria Werbowy return to fashion with a minimal luxe look in GG-strap bikini bottoms, photographed by David Sims.

In November 2023, De Sarno unveiled another line of styles that demonstrated his design philosophy for the Italian fashion house.

Alexander Fury referred to it as…

66

Softly-softly, pulling back from flamboyance and embellishment and colour – restricted to bold monochrome and a jolt of that becoming-signature Gucci Rosso Ancora… superlative Italian tailoring as a foundation for a modern man's wardrobe rooted in sartorial precision with a definitive formal slant.

AnOther Magazine, November 2023.

99

Despite the star-studded movements from De Sarno in his first few months at Gucci, he has been clear that he longs to highlight young and fresh talent that may not otherwise find themselves in the spotlight.

> "De Sarno's Gucci is closer to Tom Ford's, with the upfront sex appeal of those 60s-by-way-of-the-90s shapes and straight riffs on Ford hits, like the white going-out top trimmed in neat rows of crystals that he paired with slouchy faded blue jeans and an embellished Jackie bag."

Nicole Phelps

Vogue, September 2023.

I want people to fall in love with Gucci again.

Sabato De Sarno

Vogue, 2023.

Elegant and refined, young and bold, going back to the House's century-old roots while staying true to modern standards.

Andrea Sacal

On De Sarno's stark departure from Michele's Gucci, and a refocusing on looks that aligned closer with Ford's fashion takes, *Hypebeast*, 2023.

De Sarno has been true to his word through actions such as commissioning a Gucci art book dedicated to showcasing the work of recent graduates from Milan's fine art university, Accademia di Brera.

He has also set out to hire
plenty of fresh faces for the
runway, telling *i-D*

"

I wanted to give the opportunity
to a young girl to be a model for
a big name like Gucci… It could
change their life.

"

Sabato De Sarno

i-D, November 2023.

As of 2023, it's estimated that Gucci has been mentioned in some 22,705* songs, including notable tracks by artists such as Foxy Brown, Amy Winehouse and the rap duo Outkast.

*According to the Italian music data company Musixmatch, the number of songs that were produced all over the world over the last 100 years, since 1921.

I want women to wear my clothes
and feel beautiful, comfortable
and secure – for them to announce
themselves in the way they want.
I like it when you see the humans
behind the looks.

Sabato De Sarno

i-D, November 2023.

"

Shifting the pendulum from the maximalism and kitsch that was rampant during Alessandro Michele's era, Sabato de Sarno takes Gucci back to its essence of simplicity and chic Italian style.

"

Janelle Sessoms

L'Officiel, 2023.

De Sarno has made it clear that his vision for Gucci steps away from the brightness and boldness of Michele's Gucci and leans toward clean lines and a refined Italian approach.

How will that impact Gucci's place in the fashion world?

Time will tell.

Gucci inhabits a magical world and
I love stepping into it and getting
to be a part of it.

Miley Cyrus

Glamour, 2022.